Practical
Fish & Seafood

p^3

This is a P³ Publishing Book
This edition published in 2004

P³ Publishing
Queen Street House
4 Queen Street
Bath BA1 1HE, UK

ISBN: 1-40543-275-6

Printed in China

NOTE

Cup measurements in this book are for American cups.
This book also uses imperial and metric measurements. Follow the same units
of measurement throughout; do not mix imperial and metric.
All spoon measurements are level: teaspoons are assumed to be 5 ml, and
tablespoons are assumed to be 15 ml. Unless otherwise stated,
milk is assumed to be whole milk, eggs and individual vegetables such as potatoes
are medium, and pepper is freshly ground black pepper.

The nutritional information provided for each recipe is per serving or per person.
Optional ingredients, variations, or serving suggestions have
not been included in the calculations. The times given for each recipe are an approximate
guide only because the preparation times may differ according to the techniques used by
different people and the cooking times may vary as a result of the type of oven used.

Recipes using raw or very lightly cooked eggs should be
avoided by infants, the elderly, pregnant women, convalescents,
and anyone suffering from an illness.

Contents

Introduction

Seafood deserves its image as a healthy food. It is rich in protein, and oily fish, such as mackerel and herring, are high in polyunsaturated fats (the type that help reduce cholesterol levels). White fish are a good source of minerals as well as low in fat, especially if poached, steamed, or lightly broiled. Shellfish have been linked with high cholesterol, but they are also low in saturated fats and it is therefore healthy to eat them in moderation. The variety of fish and shellfish is staggering. You could eat seafood just once a week for a year without having the same dish twice. Seafood is quick and easy to prepare, making it an attractive ingredient for the busy cook. Many types of fish and most shellfish are sold ready to cook and so can be prepared in minutes. Fish is very good value for money in comparison with meat because there is much less waste: no fat to trim off or gristle to cut out. Making fish a regular part of your diet therefore makes a lot of sense.

Buying fish and shellfish

Wherever you shop for fish, at your trusted local fish dealer or at a large store, these guidelines apply:

- The eyes of the fish should be clear, bright, and moist. Fish with dull, gray, or cloudy eyes should be avoided.
- The gills should be bright red or pink, not dull or gray.
- Fish should smell of the sea and nothing else. Cooked shellfish should smell fresh, with no hint of ammonia. Check the use-by date if there is one.
- If you press the fish lightly with your thumb, the flesh should spring back, leaving little or no imprint.
- The shells of hinged shellfish, such as oysters, mussels, and clams, should be tightly closed before cooking. If they are slightly open, tap them sharply. If they do not close, discard them.

Storage

You never know when fish was caught, especially if you buy it in a store, so it is best to cook it on the day you buy it. If you are not planning to eat it straight away, put it in the refrigerator and do not keep it for more than a day or two. Refrigerators are not ideal places to store fish because they tend to have a temperature of about 38°F/5°C and fish is best kept at 32°F/0°C. Put the fish into a plastic container and scatter it with ice. Cover with plastic wrap and store it in the coldest part of the refrigerator.

Firm-fleshed fish, such as turbot, Dover sole, and monkfish freeze better than less firm-fleshed fish such as sea bass, flounder, and lemon sole, but all will deteriorate relatively quickly. Oily fish freezes least successfully, but if you need to keep it for more than a day or two, freezing is the best option. Thaw it thoroughly and slowly before cooking.

Preparation

The amount of preparation your fish needs depends on where you buy it. Large stores may have a wet fish counter with a trained fish dealer on hand, while other suppliers sell their fish vacuum-packed. Many fish are sold already scaled and gutted, and are often available either whole or filleted. A fish dealer will usually do the preparation for you, for a small charge. It is cheaper, however, to buy a whole fish and prepare it yourself. It is not difficult to do and just takes some practice.

Equipment

You need little special equipment for the recipes in this book, but if you are inspired by the dishes and plan to cook more fish, any of the following may prove a worthwhile purchase. If you want

to poach whole fish, a fish kettle would be a wise investment. This is an oblong, stainless-steel pan with a lifter and a lid, available in several sizes.

A wok—a Chinese pan with a heavy, rounded bottom—is useful for sautéing and stir-frying. For deep-frying you will need a deep-frying basket, a large skillet, and a thermometer. If you like to steam fish, think about buying a double boiler, a bamboo steamer, or an electric steamer. If you intend to clean fish yourself, a good filleting knife is an essential tool. Tweezers are also useful for removing small bones.

Different cooking methods suit different fish but, as a general rule, poaching, steaming, and stewing tend to produce a more moist result than broiling, baking, or barbecuing. Drying out can be minimized, however, if the latter three methods are used at sufficiently high temperatures. This reduces moisture loss by ensuring the fish is cooked very quickly.

Poaching
The fish is immersed in a poaching liquid, which might be a court-bouillon, fish bouillon, milk, beer, or hard cider. To poach successfully, bring the liquid to a boil and as soon as it boils, remove the pan from the heat, and let the fish finish cooking in the residual warmth. This method helps to prevent overcooking and is also excellent if you want to serve the fish cold.

Steaming
Both fish and shellfish benefit from being steamed. Again, a flavored liquid can be used for the steaming, which will impart some of its flavor to the fish as it is being cooked. This method is especially good for keeping the fish moist and the flavor delicate. Steaming can be done in a fish kettle, a double boiler, or in a steamer inserted over a pan of boiling water.

Stewing
Whole fish or fish pieces can be cooked in liquid along with vegetables and other ingredients, as a stew. The fish flavors the liquid as it cooks.

Broiling
This is one of the quickest and easiest cooking methods for whole fish, steaks, or fillets. Shellfish can also be broiled, but may need halving lengthwise. For all these, the broiler must be on its highest setting and the fish cooked as close to the heat source as possible.

A barbecue grill is also very useful for cooking fish. Brush the fish with butter, oil, or a marinade before and during cooking to ensure that the flesh remains moist.

Baking and roasting
This covers all methods of cooking in the oven, including open roasting, casseroling, and en papillote. This is a good method to choose for entertaining because, once the dish is in the oven, you are free to prepare other dishes.

Deep-frying
The fish may be coated in batter, flour, or bread crumbs and deep-fried in oil. You need a large, heavy-bottomed pan or a deep-fryer. Large pieces of fish in batter are best cooked at a temperature of 350°F/180°C, which lets the fish cook without burning the batter. Fish pieces, such as goujons in bread crumbs, should be cooked at 375°F/190°C. Drain deep-fried items well on paper towels so they remain crisp.

Shallow-frying or pan-frying
This is a quick method for cooking fish and shellfish, and can take as little as 3–4 minutes. A shallow layer of oil, or butter and oil, is heated in a skillet, then the fish is added and cooked until just tender and lightly browned. A good skillet is an essential piece of equipment.

KEY	
🖐	Simplicity level 1–3 (1 easiest, 3 slightly harder)
🍲	Preparation time
🕐	Cooking time

Creamy Corn Soup

This speedy soup is a good pantry standby, made in a matter of minutes. If you prefer, you can use frozen crabsticks.

NUTRITIONAL INFORMATION

Calories	183	Sugars	.........9g
Protein	.........7g	Fat	...........6g
Carbohydrate	...26g	Saturates	.......1g

🍃 🍃 🍃

🥘 5–10 mins   🕐 20 mins

SERVES 4

I N G R E D I E N T S

1 tbsp vegetable oil

3 garlic cloves, crushed

1 tsp fresh gingerroot, grated

3 cups chicken bouillon

13 oz/375 g canned creamed corn

1 tbsp Thai fish sauce

6 oz/175 g canned white crab meat, drained

1 egg

salt and pepper

TO GARNISH

fresh cilantro, shredded

paprika

1 Heat the oil in a large pan and add the garlic. Cook for about 1 minute, stirring constantly.

2 Add the ginger to the pan, then stir in the bouillon and creamed corn. Bring the soup to a boil.

3 Stir in the fish sauce and crab meat. Season with salt and pepper, then return the soup to a boil.

4 Beat the egg, then stir lightly into the soup so that it sets into long strands. Simmer gently for about 30 seconds.

5 Ladle the soup into bowls and serve hot, garnished with shredded cilantro and with paprika sprinkled over.

COOK'S TIP

To give the soup an extra-rich flavor for a special occasion, stir in 1 tablespoon of dry sherry or rice wine just before you ladle it into bowls.

Seafood Chowder

Mussels, an economical choice at the fish store, give essential flavor to this soup. The proportions of fish and shrimp are flexible.

NUTRITIONAL INFORMATION

Calories	449	Sugars	. . . . .4g
Protein	. . . . .34g	Fat	. . . . .27g
Carbohydrate	. . .18g	Saturates	. . . . . .16g

30 mins   40 mins

SERVES 6

INGREDIENTS

2 lb 4 oz/1 kg mussels

4 tbsp all-purpose flour

6⅓ cups fish bouillon

1 tbsp butter

1 large onion, finely chopped

12 oz/350 g skinless white fish fillets, such as cod, sole, or haddock

7 oz/200 g cooked or raw peeled shrimp

1¼ cups whipping cream or heavy cream

salt and pepper

fresh dill, snipped, to garnish

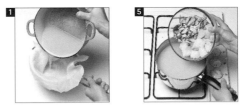

1 Discard any broken mussels and those with open shells. Rinse, and pull off any "beards". Use a knife to scrape off any barnacles under cold running water. Put the mussels in a large, heavy-bottomed pan with a little water. Cover tightly and cook over high heat for 4 minutes, or until the mussels open, shaking the pan occasionally. Remove the mussels from their shells, adding any juices to the cooking liquid. Strain through a cheesecloth-lined strainer and reserve.

2 Put the flour in a mixing bowl and very slowly whisk in enough bouillon to make a thick paste. Whisk in a little more bouillon to make a smooth liquid.

3 Melt the butter in a heavy-bottomed pan over medium-low heat. Add the onion, cover, and cook for about 5 minutes, stirring frequently, until it softens.

4 Add the remaining fish bouillon and bring to a boil. Slowly whisk in the flour mixture. Add the mussel cooking liquid. Season. Lower the heat and simmer, partially covered, for 15 minutes.

5 Add the fish and shellfish and simmer, stirring occasionally, for about 5 minutes, or until the fish is cooked and begins to flake.

6 Stir in the shrimp and cream. Taste and adjust the seasoning. Simmer for a few minutes more to heat through. Ladle into warm bowls, sprinkle the soup with fresh dill, and serve.

Salmon & Leek Soup

Salmon is a favorite with almost everyone. This delicately flavored and pretty soup is perfect for entertaining.

NUTRITIONAL INFORMATION

Calories 338	Sugars 7g	
Protein . . . .:.19g	Fat 22g	
Carbohydrate . . .17g	Saturates 8g	

10–15 mins   40 mins

SERVES 4

I N G R E D I E N T S

1 tbsp olive oil

1 large onion, finely chopped

3 large leeks, including green parts,
   thinly sliced

1 potato, finely diced

scant 2 cups fish bouillon

3 cups water

1 bay leaf

10½ oz/300 g skinless salmon fillet, cut into
   ½-inch/1-cm cubes

5 tbsp heavy cream

fresh lemon juice (optional)

salt and pepper

fresh chervil or parsley, snipped, to garnish

1 Heat the oil in a heavy-bottomed pan over medium heat. Add the onion and leeks and cook for about 3 minutes until they begin to soften.

2 Add the potato, bouillon, water, and bay leaf with a large pinch of salt. Bring to a boil, lower the heat, cover, and cook gently for about 25 minutes, until the vegetables are tender. Remove and discard the bay leaf.

3 Let the soup cool slightly, then transfer about half of it to a blender or food processor and puree until smooth. (If using a food processor, strain off the cooking liquid and reserve. Puree half the soup solids with enough cooking liquid to moisten them, then combine with the remaining liquid.)

4 Return the pureed soup to the pan and stir to blend. Reheat gently over medium-low heat.

5 Season the salmon with salt and pepper and add to the soup. Continue cooking for about 5 minutes, stirring occasionally, until the fish is tender and starts to break up. Stir in the cream, taste and adjust the seasoning, adding a little lemon juice if desired. Ladle into warm bowls, sprinkle with chervil or parsley, and serve.

Saffron Fish Soup

This elegant soup makes a good dinner-party appetizer. To make planning easier, the saffron-flavored soup base can be made ahead of time.

NUTRITIONAL INFORMATION

Calories	329	Sugars	.........8g
Protein	........19g	Fat	..........18g
Carbohydrate	...17g	Saturates	......11g

10–15 mins   40 mins

SERVES 4

I N G R E D I E N T S

2 tsp butter

1 onion, finely chopped

1 leek, thinly sliced

1 carrot, thinly sliced

4 tbsp white rice

pinch of saffron threads

½ cup dry white wine

4¼ cups fish bouillon

½ cup heavy cream

12 oz/350 g skinless white fish fillet, such as cod, haddock, or monkfish, cut into ½-inch/1-cm cubes

4 tomatoes, skinned, seeded, and chopped

3 tbsp snipped fresh chives

salt and pepper

1 Put the butter in a pan and melt over medium heat. Add the chopped onion, and sliced leek and carrot. Cook for 3–4 minutes, stirring frequently, until the onion is soft.

2 Add the rice, saffron, wine, and bouillon, bring just to a boil, and reduce the heat to low. Season with salt and pepper. Cover and simmer for 20 minutes, or until the rice and vegetables are soft.

3 Transfer the soup to a blender and puree until smooth, working in batches if necessary. (If using a food processor, strain off the cooking liquid and reserve. Puree the soup solids with enough cooking liquid to moisten them, then combine with the remaining liquid.)

4 Return the soup to the pan, stir in the cream, and simmer over low heat for a few minutes until heated through, stirring occasionally.

5 Season the fish and add, with the tomatoes, to the simmering soup. Cook for 3–5 minutes, or until the fish is just tender.

6 Stir in most of the chives. Taste the soup and adjust the seasoning, if necessary. Ladle the soup into warm shallow bowls, sprinkle the remaining chives on top, and serve.

Breton Fish Soup

Fishermen's soups are variable, depending on the season and the catch.
Monkfish has a texture like lobster, but tender cod is equally appealing.

NUTRITIONAL INFORMATION

Calories 103	Sugars 1.5g	
Protein 5.2g	Fat 6.3g	
Carbohydrate . . .6.6g	Saturates 3.8g	

5–10 mins   40 mins

SERVES 4

INGREDIENTS

2 tsp butter

1 large leek, thinly sliced

2 shallots, finely chopped

1¼ cups hard cider

½ cup fish bouillon

9 oz/250 g potatoes, diced

1 bay leaf

4 tbsp all-purpose flour

¾ cup milk

¾ cup heavy cream

2 oz/55 g fresh sorrel leaves

12 oz/350 g skinless monkfish or cod fillet,
   cut into 1-inch/2.5-cm pieces

salt and pepper

1 Melt the butter in a large pan over medium-low heat. Add the leek and shallots and then cook for about 5 minutes, stirring frequently, until they start to soften. Add the hard cider and bring to a boil.

2 Stir in the bouillon, potatoes, and bay leaf with a large pinch of salt (unless the bouillon is salty), and bring back to a boil. Lower the heat, cover the pan, and cook the soup gently for 10 minutes.

3 Put the flour in a small bowl and very slowly whisk in a few tablespoons of the milk to make a thick paste. Stir in more milk, if needed, to make a smooth liquid.

4 Adjust the heat so that the soup bubbles gently. Stir in the flour mixture and cook, stirring frequently, for 5 minutes. Add the remaining milk and half the cream. Continue cooking for about 10 minutes, until the potatoes are tender.

5 Finely chop the sorrel and combine with the remaining cream. (If using a food processor, add the sorrel and chop, then add the cream and process briefly.)

6 Stir the sorrel cream into the soup and add the fish. Continue cooking, stirring occasionally, for about 3 minutes, until the monkfish stiffens or the cod just begins to flake. Taste the soup and adjust the seasoning, if necessary. Ladle into warm bowls and serve.

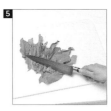

COOK'S TIP

Be careful not to overcook the fish, otherwise tender fish, such as cod, breaks up into smaller and smaller flakes, and firm fish, such as monkfish, can become tough.

Skate & Spinach Salad

This colorful fish salad makes a satisfying entrée. Skate should smell fresh, so if a fish has a strong odor of ammonia do not use it.

NUTRITIONAL INFORMATION

Calories 316	Sugars 18g	
Protein 32g	Fat 13g	
Carbohydrate . . .18g	Saturates 1g	

10 mins   40 mins

SERVES 4

I N G R E D I E N T S

1 lb 9 oz/700 g skate wings, trimmed

2 sprigs fresh rosemary

1 fresh or dried bay leaf

1 tbsp black peppercorns

1 lemon, cut into fourths

1 lb/450 g baby spinach leaves

1 tbsp olive oil

1 small red onion, thinly sliced

2 garlic cloves, crushed

½ tsp chili flakes

1¾ oz/50 g pine nuts, lightly toasted

1¾ oz/50 g raisins

1 tbsp brown sugar

2 tbsp chopped fresh parsley

1 Put the skate wings into a large pan with the rosemary, bay leaf, peppercorns, and lemon pieces. Cover with cold water and bring to a boil. Simmer, covered, for 4–5 minutes, until the flesh begins to come away from the cartilage. Remove from the heat and let stand for 15 minutes.

2 Lift the fish from the poaching water and remove the flesh by shredding it off. Set aside.

3 In a clean pan, cook the spinach (with just the water that clings to the leaves after washing) over high heat for 30 seconds, until just wilted. Drain, refresh under cold water, and drain well again. Squeeze out excess water and set aside.

4 Heat the olive oil in a large, deep skillet. Add the red onion and cook for 3–4 minutes, until softened but not browned. Add the garlic, chili flakes, pine nuts, raisins, and sugar. Cook the mixture for 1–2 minutes, then add the spinach and toss for 1 minute until heated through.

5 Gently fold in the skate and cook for another minute. Season well.

6 Divide the salad between 4 serving plates and sprinkle with the chopped parsley. Serve immediately.

Smoked Mackerel Pâté

This is a quick and easy pâté with plenty of flavor. It originates from Goa, on the west coast of India, an area famous for its seafood.

NUTRITIONAL INFORMATION

Calories 316	Sugars 3g
Protein 13g	Fat 23g
Carbohydrate . . .14g	Saturates 8g

🐟 🐟 🐟

25–30 mins, plus refrigeration time — 5–10 mins

SERVES 4

I N G R E D I E N T S

7 oz/200 g smoked mackerel fillet

1 small, hot green chile, seeded and chopped

1 garlic clove, chopped

3 tbsp fresh cilantro leaves

⅔ cup sour cream

1 small red onion, chopped

2 tbsp lime juice

4 slices white bread, crusts removed

salt and pepper

1 Skin and flake the mackerel fillet, removing any small bones. Put the flesh in the bowl of a food processor along with the chile, garlic, cilantro, and sour cream. Blend until smooth.

2 Transfer the mixture to a bowl and mix in the onion and lime juice. Season to taste. The pâté will seem very soft at this stage but will firm up in the refrigerator. Refrigerate for several hours, or overnight if possible.

3 The pâté is served with melba toast. To make it, place the trimmed bread slices under a preheated medium broiler and toast lightly on both sides. Split each piece in half horizontally, then cut across diagonally to form 4 triangles per slice.

4 Put the melba toast triangles, untoasted side up, under the broiler and toast them until they are golden and curled at the edges. Serve the toast warm or cold with the pâté.

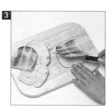

Thai Fishcakes

These little fishcakes are very popular in Thailand as street food, and make a perfect snack. Alternatively, serve them as an appetizer.

NUTRITIONAL INFORMATION	
Calories 205	Sugars 6g
Protein 17g	Fat 12g
Carbohydrate 7g	Saturates 2g

5–10 mins   30–40 mins

SERVES 4–5

INGREDIENTS

12 oz/350 g white fish fillet without skin, such as cod or haddock

1 tbsp Thai fish sauce

2 tsp Thai red curry paste

1 tbsp lime juice

1 garlic clove, crushed

4 dried kaffir lime leaves, crumbled

1 egg white

3 tbsp chopped fresh cilantro

vegetable oil, for cooking

salt and pepper

fresh salad greens, to serve

PEANUT DIP

1 small red chile

1 tbsp light soy sauce

1 tbsp lime juice

1 tbsp brown sugar

3 tbsp chunky peanut butter

4 tbsp coconut milk

1 Put the fish fillet in a food processor with the fish sauce, red curry paste, lime juice, garlic, lime leaves, and egg white, and process the ingredients until a smooth paste forms.

2 Stir in the fresh cilantro and quickly process the paste again until it is mixed. Divide the fish mixture into about 8–10 pieces and roll into balls, then flatten the balls to make round patties and set them aside.

3 To make the peanut dip, halve and seed the chile, then chop finely. Place in a small pan with the remaining dip ingredients and heat gently, stirring constantly, until blended. Season to taste.

4 Heat the oil in a skillet and cook the fishcakes for 3–4 minutes on each side, until golden brown (you may need to do this in batches). Drain on paper towels and serve hot on a bed of salad greens with the peanut dip.

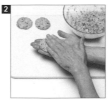

Gravlax

You need two pieces of salmon fillet approximately the same size for this dish. Ask your fish dealer to remove all the bones and scale the fish.

NUTRITIONAL INFORMATION	
Calories 608	Sugars 11g
Protein 37g	Fat 34g
Carbohydrate ...41g	Saturates 14g

30–40 mins, plus
2 days chilling   0 mins

SERVES 6

I N G R E D I E N T S

2 salmon fillets, about 1 lb/450 g each, skin left on

6 tbsp coarsely chopped fresh dill

4 oz/115 g sea salt

¼ cup sugar

1 tbsp coarsely crushed white peppercorns

12 slices brown bread, buttered, to serve

G A R N I S H

lemon slices

sprigs of fresh dill

1 Rinse the salmon fillets and dry with paper towels. Put one fillet, skin-side down, in a nonmetallic dish.

2 Mix together the dill, sea salt, sugar, and peppercorns. Spread this mixture over the first fillet of fish and place the second fillet, skin-side up, on top. Put a plate, the same size as the fish, on top and put a weight on the plate (3 or 4 cans of tomatoes or similar will do).

3 Refrigerate for 2 days, turning the salmon fillets about every 12 hours and basting with any juices that have come out of the fish.

4 Remove the salmon from the brine and slice thinly, without slicing the skin, as you would smoked salmon. Cut the brown bread into triangles and serve with the salmon. Garnish with lemon wedges and sprigs of fresh dill.

COOK'S TIP

You can brush the marinade off the salmon before slicing, but the line of green along the edge of the salmon is quite attractive and, of course, full of flavor.

Thai-Style Crab Sandwich

A hearty, open sandwich, topped with a classic flavor combination—
crab with avocado and ginger. Perfect for a light summer lunch.

NUTRITIONAL INFORMATION

Calories 768	Sugars 3g	
Protein 26g	Fat 49g	
Carbohydrate . . .58g	Saturates 8g	

40 mins   0 mins

SERVES 2

I N G R E D I E N T S

2 tbsp lime juice

¾-inch/2-cm piece fresh gingerroot, grated

¾-inch/2-cm piece lemongrass,
  finely chopped

5 tbsp mayonnaise

2 large slices crusty bread

1 ripe avocado

¾ cup cooked crab meat

freshly ground black pepper

sprigs of fresh cilantro, to garnish

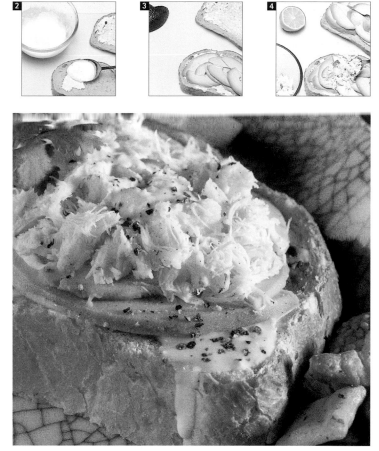

COOK'S TIP

To make mayonnaise flavored
with lime and ginger, place 2 egg
yolks, 1 tablespoon lime juice, and
½ teaspoon grated gingerroot in a
blender. With the motor running,
gradually add 1¼ cups olive oil,
drop by drop, until the mixture
is thick and smooth. Season
with salt and pepper.

1 Mix half the lime juice with the
gingerroot and lemongrass. Add
1 tablespoon of mayonnaise and mix well.

2 Spread 1 tablespoon of mayonnaise
smoothly over each slice of bread.

3 Halve the avocado and remove the
pit. Peel and slice the flesh thinly,
then arrange the slices on the bread.
Sprinkle with lime juice.

4 Spoon the crab meat over the
avocado, then add the remaining
lime juice. Spoon over the remaining
mayonnaise, season with freshly ground
black pepper, top with cilantro sprigs, and
serve immediately.

Swordfish or Tuna Fajitas

Fajitas are usually made with chicken or lamb but using a firm fish like swordfish or tuna works very well.

NUTRITIONAL INFORMATION

Calories	766	Sugars 12g
Protein	........52g	Fat 36g
Carbohydrate	...63g	Saturates 10g

🥬 ⏱ 30 mins, plus 1–2 hrs marinating   20 mins

SERVES 4

I N G R E D I E N T S

3 tbsp olive oil

2 tsp chili powder

1 tsp ground cumin

pinch cayenne pepper

1 garlic clove, crushed

2 lb/900 g swordfish or tuna steaks

1 red bell pepper, seeded and thinly sliced

1 yellow bell pepper, seeded and thinly sliced

2 zucchini, cut into batons

1 large onion, thinly sliced

12 soft flour tortillas

1 tbsp lemon juice

3 tbsp chopped fresh cilantro

salt and pepper

⅔ cup sour cream, to serve

G U A C A M O L E

1 large avocado

1 tomato, skinned, seeded, and diced

1 garlic clove, crushed

dash of Tabasco

2 tbsp lemon juice

salt and pepper

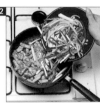
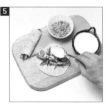

1 In a bowl, mix together the oil, chili powder, cumin, cayenne, and garlic. Cut the fish into chunks and mix with the marinade. Set aside for 1–2 hours.

2 Heat a large skillet until hot. Put in the fish and its marinade and cook for 2 minutes, stirring occasionally, until the fish begins to brown. Add the bell peppers, zucchini, and onion and cook for another 5 minutes, until the vegetables have softened but all are still firm.

3 Meanwhile, gently warm the tortillas in an oven or microwave.

4 To make the guacamole, mash the avocado in a bowl. Stir in the tomato, garlic, Tabasco, lemon juice, and seasoning.

5 Add the lemon juice, cilantro, and seasoning to the vegetable mix. Spoon some of the mixture on the warmed tortillas. Top each one with guacamole and a spoonful of sour cream and roll up.

Steamed Yellow Fish Fillets

Thailand has an abundance of fresh fish, which is an important part of the local diet. Dishes such as these steamed fillets are popular.

NUTRITIONAL INFORMATION

Calories 165	Sugars 1g	
Protein 23g	Fat 2g	
Carbohydrate ...13g	Saturates 1g	

🌶 🌶 🌶

🥔 40 mins   🕐 15 mins

SERVES 3-4

I N G R E D I E N T S

1 lb 2 oz/500 g firm fish fillets, such as red snapper, sole, or monkfish

1 dried red bird's-eye chile

1 small onion, chopped

3 garlic cloves, chopped

2 sprigs fresh cilantro

1 tsp coriander seeds

½ tsp turmeric

½ tsp freshly ground black pepper

1 tbsp Thai fish sauce

2 tbsp coconut milk

1 small egg, beaten

2 tbsp rice flour

strips of red and green chile, to garnish

soy sauce, to serve

1 Remove any skin from the fish and cut the fillets diagonally into long ¾-inch/2-cm wide strips.

2 Place the dried chile in a mortar. Add the onion, garlic, cilantro, and coriander seeds and grind with a pestle until they make a smooth paste.

3 Add the turmeric, black pepper, fish sauce, coconut milk, and beaten egg, and stir well to mix evenly.

4 Dip the fish strips into the paste mixture, then into the rice flour to coat lightly.

5 Bring the water in a steamer to a boil, then arrange the fish strips in the top of the steamer. Cover and steam for about 12–15 minutes, until the fish is just firm.

6 Serve the fish with soy sauce and an accompaniment of stir-fried vegetables or salad.

COOK'S TIP

If you don't have a steamer, improvise by placing a large metal colander over a large pan of boiling water and cover with an upturned plate to enclose the fish as it steams.

Cotriade

This is a rich French stew of fish and vegetables, flavored with saffron and herbs. The fish and vegetables, and the soup, are served separately.

NUTRITIONAL INFORMATION

Calories 81   Sugars 0.9g
Protein . . . . .7.4g   Fat 3.9g
Carbohydrate . . .3.8g   Saturates 1.1g

15 mins   40 mins

SERVES 6

INGREDIENTS

large pinch saffron

2½ cups hot fish bouillon

1 tbsp olive oil

2 tbsp butter

1 onion, sliced

2 garlic cloves, chopped

1 leek, sliced

1 small fennel bulb, finely sliced

1 lb/450 g potatoes, cut into chunks

⅔ cup dry white wine

1 tbsp fresh thyme leaves

2 bay leaves

4 ripe tomatoes, skinned and chopped

2 lb/900 g mixed fish such as haddock,
   hake, mackerel, or red snapper,
   coarsely chopped

2 tbsp chopped fresh parsley

salt and pepper

lemon slices and crusty bread, to serve

1 Using a mortar and pestle, crush the saffron and add it to the fish bouillon. Stir the mixture and let stand to infuse for at least 10 minutes.

2 In a large pan, heat the oil and butter together. Add the onion and cook gently for 4–5 minutes, until softened. Add the garlic, leek, fennel, and potatoes. Cover and cook for another 10–15 minutes, until the vegetables have softened.

3 Add the wine and simmer rapidly for 3–4 minutes, until it has reduced by half. Add the thyme, bay leaves, and tomatoes and stir well. Add the saffron-infused bouillon. Bring to a boil, cover, and simmer gently for 15 minutes, until the vegetables are tender.

4 Add the fish, return to a boil, and simmer for another 3–4 minutes, until the fish is tender. Add the parsley and season to taste. Using a slotted spoon, remove the fish and vegetables to a warmed serving dish. Serve the soup with lemon slices and plenty of crusty bread.

Basque Tuna Stew

Although versions of this stew are eaten throughout Spain, it originated in the northern Basque region.

NUTRITIONAL INFORMATION

Calories	110	Sugars	.........8g
Protein	........10g	Fat	...........2g
Carbohydrate	...13g	Saturates	.......0g

10–15 mins   40 mins

SERVES 4

INGREDIENTS

5 tbsp olive oil

1 large onion, chopped

2 garlic cloves, chopped

7 oz/200 g canned chopped tomatoes

1 lb 9 oz/700 g potatoes, cut into 2-inch/5-cm chunks

3 green bell peppers, seeded and coarsely chopped

1¼ cups cold water

2 lb/900 g fresh tuna, cut into chunks

4 slices crusty white bread

salt and pepper

VARIATION

Substitute any very firm-fleshed fish, such as shark or swordfish, for the tuna used in this recipe.

1 Heat 2 tablespoons of the olive oil in a pan and add the onion. Cook for 8–10 minutes, until soft and brown. Add the garlic and cook for another minute, then add the tomatoes. Cover and simmer for 30 minutes, until thickened.

2 Meanwhile, in a clean pan, mix together the potatoes and bell peppers. Add the water (which should just cover the vegetables). Bring to a boil and simmer for 15 minutes, until the potatoes are almost cooked through.

3 Add the tuna and the tomato mixture to the potatoes and bell peppers and season. Cover the pan and simmer for 6–8 minutes, until the tuna is tender.

4 Meanwhile, heat the remaining oil in a large skillet over medium heat and add the bread slices. Cook them on both sides until golden. Drain on paper towels. Serve with the stew.

Sardines with Pesto

This is a very quick and tasty midweek supper dish. Use a good-quality ready-made pesto for an even speedier meal.

NUTRITIONAL INFORMATION

Calories 617   Sugars 0.1g
Protein . . . . .27g   Fat 56g
Carbohydrate . . . .1g   Saturates 11g

🦀 🦀 🦀

🧊 30 mins   🕐 10 mins

SERVES 4

I N G R E D I E N T S

16 large sardines, scaled and gutted

2 loosely packed cups fresh basil leaves

2 garlic cloves, crushed

2 tbsp pine nuts, toasted

½ cup freshly grated Parmesan cheese

⅔ cup olive oil

salt and pepper

lemon slices, to serve

1 Wash and dry the sardines and arrange on a broiler pan.

2 Put the basil leaves, garlic, and pine nuts in a food processor. Blend until finely chopped. Scrape the mixture out of the food processor, put in a bowl, and stir in the Parmesan cheese and olive oil. Season to taste.

3 Spread a little of the pesto sauce over one side of the sardines and place under a preheated hot broiler for 3 minutes. Turn the fish, spread with more pesto, and broil for another 3 minutes, until the sardines are cooked.

4 Serve immediately with extra pesto and lemon slices.

VARIATION
This treatment will also work well with other small oily fish such as herrings and pilchards.

Seared Tuna Steaks

Meaty tuna steaks have enough flavor to stand up to the robust taste of anchovies. Serve this with pan-fried potatoes or a mixed rice dish.

NUTRITIONAL INFORMATION		
Calories ...... .564	Sugars 0g	
Protein 55g	Fat .... .38g	
Carbohydrate 0g	Saturates ..... .19g	

35 mins   5 mins

SERVES 4

I N G R E D I E N T S

olive oil

4 thick tuna steaks, each about 8 oz/225 g and ¾ inch/2 cm thick

salt and pepper

ANCHOVY BUTTER

8 anchovy fillets in oil, drained

4 scallions, finely chopped

1 tbsp finely grated orange zest

½ cup sweet butter, softened

¼ tsp lemon juice

pepper

TO GARNISH

sprigs of fresh flatleaf parsley

strips of orange zest

1 To make the anchovy butter, chop the anchovies very finely and put them in a bowl with the scallions, orange zest, and softened butter. Beat well until all the ingredients are blended. Season with lemon juice and pepper to taste.

2 Place the flavored butter on a sheet of baking parchment and then roll it up into a log shape. Fold over the ends of the paper carefully to seal in the butter, then place the package in the freezer for about 15 minutes to firm.

3 Heat a ridged grill pan over high heat. Lightly brush with olive oil, add the tuna steaks, and cook for 2 minutes, in batches if necessary. Turn the steaks over and cook for 2 more minutes for rare, or up to 4 minutes for well done. Season to taste with salt and pepper.

4 Transfer the fish to a warm plate and put 2 thin slices of anchovy butter on each of the tuna steaks. Garnish with fresh parsley sprigs and orange zest, and serve the dish at once.

VARIATION
If you particularly like hot, spicy food, add a pinch of dried chili flakes to the butter mixture.

Shrimp Rostis

These crisp little vegetable and shrimp cakes make an ideal light lunch or supper, accompanied by a salad.

NUTRITIONAL INFORMATION

Calories	445	Sugars	. . . . .9g
Protein	. . . . .19g	Fat	. . . . .29g
Carbohydrate	. . .29g	Saturates	. . . . . . .4g

🦐 🦐 🦐

🥔 10 mins   🕐 1 hr

SERVES 4

I N G R E D I E N T S

12 oz/350 g potatoes

12 oz/350 g celeriac

1 carrot

½ small onion

8 oz/225 g shrimp, cooked and peeled, thawed if frozen and well drained on paper towels

2½ tbsp all-purpose flour

1 egg, lightly beaten

vegetable oil, for cooking

salt and pepper

C H E R R Y   T O M A T O   S A L S A

8 oz/225 g mixed cherry tomatoes such as baby plum, yellow, orange, or pear, cut into fourths

½ small mango, finely diced

1 red chile, seeded and finely chopped

½ small red onion, finely chopped

1 tbsp chopped fresh cilantro

1 tbsp chopped fresh chives

2 tbsp olive oil

2 tsp lemon juice

salt and pepper

1 For the salsa, mix the tomatoes in a bowl with the mango, chile, onion, cilantro, chives, olive oil, lemon juice, and seasoning. Set aside for the flavors to infuse.

2 Using a food processor or the fine blade of a box grater, finely grate the potatoes, celeriac, carrot, and onion. Mix together in a bowl with the shrimp, flour, and egg. Season well and set aside.

3 Divide the shrimp mixture into eight equal pieces. Press each piece into a greased 4-inch/10-cm cookie cutter (if you have only one cutter, you can simply shape the rostis individually).

4 In a large skillet, heat a shallow layer of oil. When hot, transfer the vegetable cakes, still in the cutters if possible, to the skillet, in batches if necessary. When the oil sizzles underneath, remove the cutter. Cook gently, pressing down with a spatula, for 6 0 minutes on each side, until crisp and browned and the vegetables are tender. Drain on paper towels and keep warm in a preheated oven. Serve the rostis hot with the tomato salsa.

Seafood Lasagna

A rich dish of layers of pasta, with seafood and mushrooms in a tomato sauce, topped with béchamel sauce, and baked until golden.

NUTRITIONAL INFORMATION

Calories	790	Sugars	.......23g
Protein	........55g	Fat	.........32g
Carbohydrate	...74g	Saturates	......19g

🍽 🍽 🍽

❄ 30 mins   ⏲ 1 hr 20 mins

SERVES 6

I N G R E D I E N T S

4 tbsp butter, plus extra for greasing

6 tbsp flour

1 tsp mustard powder

2½ cups milk

2 tbsp olive oil

1 onion, chopped

2 garlic cloves, finely chopped

1 tbsp fresh thyme leaves

6 cups mixed mushrooms, sliced

⅔ cup white wine

14 oz/400 g canned chopped tomatoes

1 lb/450 g skinless mixed white fish fillets, cubed

8 oz/225 g fresh scallops, trimmed

4–6 sheets fresh lasagna

8 oz/225 g mozzarella cheese, drained and chopped

salt and pepper

1 Melt the butter in a pan. Add the flour and mustard powder and stir until smooth. Simmer gently for 2 minutes without coloring. Gradually stir in the milk, whisking until smooth. Bring to a boil and simmer for 2 minutes. Remove from the heat, transfer to a bowl, and cover the surface of the sauce with plastic wrap to prevent a skin from forming. Set aside.

2 Heat the oil in a skillet and add the onion, garlic, and thyme. Cook gently for 5 minutes, until softened. Add the mushrooms and cook for an additional 5 minutes, until softened. Stir in the wine and boil rapidly, until nearly evaporated. Stir in the tomatoes. Bring to a boil and simmer, covered, for 15 minutes. Season and set aside.

3 Grease a lasagna dish. Spoon half of the tomato sauce in the dish and top with half the fish and scallops.

4 Layer half of the lasagna over the fish, pour over half the white sauce, and then add half of the mozzarella. Repeat these layers, finishing with the white sauce and mozzarella.

5 Bake the lasagna in a preheated oven at 400°F/200°C for 35–40 minutes, until the top is bubbling and golden and the fish is cooked through. Remove the dish from the oven and let stand on a heat-resistant counter or mat for about 10 minutes before serving.

Thai Noodles

This classic Thai noodle dish is flavored with fish sauce, roasted peanuts, and jumbo shrimp.

NUTRITIONAL INFORMATION

Calories	344	Sugars	.........2g
Protein	........21g	Fat	..........17g
Carbohydrate	...27g	Saturates	.......2g

15 mins   30 mins

SERVES 4

INGREDIENTS

12 oz/350 g jumbo shrimp, peeled

4 oz/115 g flat rice noodles or
  rice vermicelli

4 tbsp vegetable oil

2 garlic cloves, finely chopped

1 egg

2 tbsp lemon juice

1½ tbsp Thai fish sauce

½ tsp sugar

2 tbsp chopped roasted peanuts

1¾ oz/50 g fresh bean sprouts

½ tsp cayenne pepper

2 scallions, cut into 1-inch/2.5-cm pieces

1 tbsp chopped fresh cilantro

lemon wedges, to serve

VARIATION

This is a basic dish to which lots of different cooked seafood could be added. Cooked squid rings, mussels, and langoustines would all work just as well.

1 Drain the shrimp on paper towels to remove excess moisture. Set aside. Cook the rice noodles or rice vermicelli according to the package instructions. Drain well and set aside.

2 Heat the oil in a wok or large skillet and then add the chopped garlic. Cook until the garlic is just golden. Add the egg and stir quickly to break it up. Cook for a few seconds.

3 Add the shrimp and noodles, scraping down the sides of the pan to ensure they mix with the egg and garlic.

4 Add the lemon juice, fish sauce, sugar, half the peanuts and bean sprouts, and all the cayenne pepper and scallions, stirring quickly all the time. Cook over high heat for another 4 minutes, until everything is heated through.

5 Turn onto serving plates. Top with the remaining peanuts and bean sprouts and sprinkle with the cilantro. Serve with lemon wedges.

Kedgeree

Originally, kedgeree or *khichri* was a Hindu dish of rice and lentils, varied with fish or meat in all kinds of ways.

NUTRITIONAL INFORMATION

Calories ....457 Sugars 3g
Protein ....33g Fat 18g
Carbohydrate ...40g Saturates 6g

10–15 mins   30 mins

SERVES 4

INGREDIENTS

1 lb/450 g undyed smoked haddock fillet

2 tbsp olive oil

1 large onion, chopped

2 garlic cloves, finely chopped

½ tsp ground turmeric

½ tsp ground cumin

1 tsp ground coriander

¾ cup basmati rice

4 medium eggs

2 tbsp butter

1 tbsp chopped fresh parsley

TO SERVE

lemon wedges

mango chutney

1 Pour boiling water over the haddock fillet and let stand for 10 minutes. Lift the fish from the cooking water, discard the skin and bones, and flake the fish. Set aside. Reserve the cooking water.

2 Heat the oil in a large pan and add the onion. Cook for 10 minutes over medium heat, until starting to brown. Add the garlic and cook for an additional 30 seconds. Add the turmeric, cumin, and coriander and stir-fry for 30 seconds, until the spices smell fragrant. Add the rice and stir well.

3 Measure out 1½ cups of the haddock cooking water and add this to the pan. Stir well and bring to a boil. Cover the pan and cook over very low heat for 12–15 minutes, until the rice is tender and the liquid is absorbed.

4 Meanwhile, bring a small pan of water to a boil and place the eggs carefully in the water. When the water has returned to a boil, cook the eggs for 8 minutes.

Drain them immediately, and refresh under cold water to stop them from cooking. Set them to one side.

5 Add the reserved pieces of haddock, the butter, and the fresh parsley to the rice. Turn the rice onto a large serving dish. Shell the hard-cooked eggs, cut them into fourths, and arrange them on top of the rice. Serve the kedgeree with lemon wedges and mango chutney.

Moules Marinières

The Spanish, French, and Italians all serve variations of this simple mussel recipe, which is universally popular. Use the freshest mussels you can find.

NUTRITIONAL INFORMATION

Calories	278	Sugars	.........6g
Protein	.......18g	Fat	.........14g
Carbohydrate	...10g	Saturates	.......2g

30 mins   25 mins

SERVES 4

I N G R E D I E N T S

4 lb 8 oz/2 kg live mussels

4 tbsp olive oil

4–6 large garlic cloves, halved

1 lb 12 oz/800 g canned chopped tomatoes

1¼ cups dry white wine

2 tbsp finely chopped fresh flatleaf parsley, plus extra to garnish

1 tbsp finely chopped fresh oregano

salt and pepper

French bread, to serve

1 Let the mussels soak in a bowl of lightly salted water for 30 minutes. Rinse them under cold, running water and lightly scrub to remove any sand from the shells. Using a small, sharp knife, remove the "beards" from the shells.

2 Discard any broken mussels or open mussels that do not shut when tapped firmly with the back of a knife. This indicates they are dead and could cause food poisoning if eaten. Rinse the mussels again, then set aside in a colander.

3 Heat the olive oil in a large pan or pot over medium-high heat. Add the garlic and cook, stirring, for about 3 minutes to flavor the oil. Using a slotted spoon, remove the garlic from the pan.

4 Add the tomatoes and their juice, the wine, parsley, and oregano, and bring to a boil, stirring. Lower the heat, cover, and simmer for 5 minutes to let the flavors blend.

5 Add the mussels, cover, and simmer for 5–8 minutes, shaking the pan regularly, until they open. Using a slotted spoon, transfer them to serving bowls, discarding any that are not open.

6 Season the sauce with salt and pepper to taste. Ladle the sauce over the mussels, sprinkle with extra parsley, and serve at once with plenty of French bread to soak up the delicious juices.

Tuna in Sweet-&-Sour Sauce

Tuna is a firm, meaty-textured fish. You can also use shark or mackerel with this rich and delicious sauce.

NUTRITIONAL INFORMATION

Calories	303	Sugars	. . . . .12g
Protein	. . . . .31g	Fat	. . . . .12g
Carbohydrate	. . .20g	Saturates	. . . . . . .3g

30 mins   20 mins

SERVES 4

INGREDIENTS

4 fresh tuna steaks, about 1 lb 2 oz/500 g total weight

¼ tsp freshly ground black pepper

2 tbsp peanut oil

1 onion, diced

1 small red bell pepper, seeded and cut into short, thin sticks

1 garlic clove, crushed

1 tbsp brown sugar

½ cucumber, seeded and cut into short, thin sticks

2 pineapple slices, diced

1 tsp fresh gingerroot, finely chopped

1 tbsp cornstarch

1½ tbsp lime juice

1 tbsp Thai fish sauce

1 cup fish bouillon

lime and cucumber slices, to garnish

1 Sprinkle the tuna steaks with black pepper on both sides and brush with a little of the oil. Heat a heavy skillet or ridged grill pan. Arrange the tuna steaks on the pan and cook for about 8 minutes, turning them over once during cooking.

2 Heat the remaining oil in another pan and cook the onion, bell pepper, and garlic gently for 3–4 minutes to soften.

3 Remove from the heat, then stir in the sugar, cucumber, pineapple slices, and chopped ginger.

4 In a separate bowl, blend the cornstarch with the lime juice and fish sauce, then stir in the bouillon and add to the pan. Stir over medium heat until boiling, then cook for 1–2 minutes, until thickened and clear.

5 Spoon the sauce over the tuna and serve garnished with slices of lime and cucumber.

Poached Rainbow Trout

This colorful dish is served cold and makes a lovely summer lunch or supper dish. If watercress is unavailable, use baby spinach instead.

NUTRITIONAL INFORMATION

Calories	99	Sugars	.......1.1g
Protein	........5.7g	Fat	.........6.3g
Carbohydrate	...3.7g	Saturates	.......1g

10 mins

1 hr 5 mins

SERVES 4

I N G R E D I E N T S

3 lb/1.3 kg rainbow trout fillets, cleaned

1 lb 9 oz/700 g new potatoes, halved

3 scallions, finely chopped

1 egg, hard-cooked and chopped

C O U R T - B O U I L L O N

$3^2/_3$ cups cold water

$3^2/_3$ cups dry white wine

3 tbsp white wine vinegar

2 large carrots, coarsely chopped

1 onion, coarsely chopped

2 celery stalks, coarsely chopped

2 leeks, coarsely chopped

2 garlic cloves, coarsely chopped

2 fresh or dried bay leaves

4 sprigs of fresh parsley

4 sprigs of fresh thyme

6 black peppercorns

1 tsp salt

M A Y O N N A I S E

1 egg yolk

1 tsp Dijon mustard

1 tsp white wine vinegar

55 g/2 oz watercress leaves, chopped

scant 1 cup light olive oil

salt and pepper

1 Place the court-bouillon ingredients in a large pan, cover, and simmer for about 30 minutes. Strain through a fine strainer into a clean pan. Bring to a boil again and simmer fast, uncovered, for 15–20 minutes, until reduced to 2½ cups.

2 Place the trout in a skillet. Add the court-bouillon and bring slowly to a boil. Remove from the heat and leave in the poaching liquid to go cold.

3 To make the mayonnaise, put the egg yolk, mustard, vinegar, watercress, and seasoning into a food processor and blend for 30 seconds, until foaming. Add the olive oil, drop by drop, until the mixture begins to thicken. Continue adding the oil in a slow stream, until incorporated. Add a little hot water if it is too thick. Season and set aside.

4 Cook the potatoes in boiling water for 12–15 minutes. Drain and refresh under cold running water. Set aside.

5 Toss the cold potatoes with the watercress mayonnaise, scallions, and hard-cooked egg.

6 Lift the fish from the poaching liquid and drain on paper towels. Carefully pull the skin away from the trout. Serve immediately with the potato salad.

Hake Steaks with Chermoula

The cooking time may seem long and indeed you could decrease it slightly if you prefer, but in Morocco they like their fish well cooked.

NUTRITIONAL INFORMATION

Calories 590	Sugars 1g
Protein 42g	Fat 46g
Carbohydrate 2g	Saturates 7g

10 mins, plus marinating

SERVES 4

INGREDIENTS

4 hake steaks, about 8 oz/225 g each

4 oz/115 g pitted green olives

MARINADE

6 tbsp finely chopped fresh cilantro

6 tbsp finely chopped fresh parsley

6 garlic cloves, crushed

1 tbsp ground cumin

1 tsp ground coriander

1 tbsp paprika

pinch cayenne pepper

⅔ cup fresh lemon juice

1¼ cups olive oil

selection of freshly cooked vegetables, to serve

1 For the marinade, combine the cilantro, parsley, garlic, cumin, coriander, paprika, cayenne, lemon juice, and olive oil.

2 Wash and dry the hake steaks and place in an ovenproof dish. Pour the marinade over the fish and let stand for at least 1 hour and preferably overnight.

3 Before cooking the hake steaks, scatter the pitted green olives over the fish and then cover the dish with aluminum foil.

4 Place the hake in a preheated oven at 325°F/160°C. Cook for approximately 35–40 minutes, until the fish is tender. Serve the steaks with a selection of freshly cooked vegetables.

VARIATION
Remove the fish from the marinade and dust with seasoned flour. Cook in oil or clarified butter, until golden. Warm through the marinade, but do not boil, and serve as a sauce with lemon slices.

Dover Sole à la Meunière

Dover sole à la meunière, or "in the style of a miller's wife," gets its name from the light dusting of flour that the fish is given before cooking.

NUTRITIONAL INFORMATION

Calories ....584 Sugars 0g
Protein ....74g Fat 29g
Carbohydrate ...10g Saturates 14g

🔥 🔥 🔥

❄ 20 mins   🕐 15 mins

SERVES 4

INGREDIENTS

4 tbsp all-purpose flour

1 tsp salt

4 Dover soles, about 14 oz/400 g each, cleaned and skinned

⅔ cup butter

3 tbsp lemon juice

1 tbsp chopped fresh parsley

¼ preserved lemon, finely chopped (optional)

salt and pepper

lemon wedges and parsley, to garnish

1 Mix the flour with the salt and place on a large plate or tray. Drop the fish into the flour, one at a time, and shake well to remove any excess. Melt 3 tablespoons of the butter in a small pan and use to brush the fish liberally all over.

2 Place under a preheated hot broiler and cook for 5 minutes on each side.

3 Meanwhile, melt the remaining butter in a small pan. Pour cold water into a bowl, large enough to take the bottom of the pan. Keep nearby.

4 Heat the butter until it turns a golden brown and begins to smell nutty.

Remove immediately from the heat and immerse the bottom of the pan in the cold water, to stop the cooking.

5 Put the fish onto individual serving plates, drizzle with the lemon juice, and sprinkle over the parsley, and preserved lemon if using. Season with salt and pepper. Pour over the browned butter and serve immediately, garnished with lemon wedges and parsley sprigs.

COOK'S TIP

If you have a large enough pan (or two) you can cook the floured fish in butter, if you prefer.

Stuffed Monkfish Tail

A very impressive-looking dish, which is very simple to prepare. The fish is stuffed with herbs and wrapped in slices of prosciutto.

NUTRITIONAL INFORMATION

Calories 154	Sugars 0g	
Protein 24g	Fat 6g	
Carbohydrate 0g	Saturates 1g	

15 mins   40 mins

SERVES 6

INGREDIENTS

1 lb 10 oz/750 g monkfish tail, skinned and trimmed

6 slices prosciutto

4 tbsp chopped fresh mixed herbs such as parsley, chives, basil, and sage

1 tsp finely grated lemon zest

2 tbsp olive oil

salt and pepper

TO SERVE

shredded stir-fried vegetables

freshly cooked new potatoes

1 Using a sharp knife, carefully cut down each side of the central bone of the monkfish to leave 2 fillets. Wash and dry the fillets.

2 Lay the prosciutto slices widthwise on a clean counter so that they overlap slightly. Lay the fish fillets lengthwise on top of the prosciutto so that the two cut sides face each other.

3 Mix together the chopped herbs and lemon zest. Season well. Pack this mixture onto the cut surface of one monkfish fillet. Press the 2 fillets together and wrap tightly with the prosciutto slices. Secure with string or toothpicks.

4 Heat the olive oil in a large, ovenproof skillet and place the fish in the skillet, seam-side down first, and brown the wrapped monkfish tail all over.

5 Transfer to a preheated oven and bake at 400°F/200°C for 25 minutes, until the fish is golden and tender. Remove from the oven and let rest for 10 minutes before slicing thickly. Serve with shredded stir-fried vegetables and freshly cooked new potatoes.

COOK'S TIP
It is possible to remove the central bone from a monkfish tail without separating the two fillets completely. This makes it easier to stuff, but takes some practice.

Swordfish à la Maltaise

The firm texture of swordfish means it is often simply broiled, but it also lends itself to this delicate technique of cooking in a paper package.

NUTRITIONAL INFORMATION

Calories	303	Sugars	........10g
Protein	........34g	Fat	..........13g
Carbohydrate	...13g	Saturates	.......3g

35 mins   30 mins

SERVES 4

INGREDIENTS

1 tbsp fennel seeds

2 tbsp fruity extra-virgin olive oil, plus extra
  for brushing and drizzling

2 large onions, thinly sliced

1 small garlic clove, crushed

4 swordfish steaks, about 6 oz/175 g each

1 large lemon, cut in half

2 large sun-ripened tomatoes,
  finely chopped

4 sprigs of fresh thyme

salt and pepper

1 Place the fennel seeds in a dry skillet over medium-high heat and toast, stirring, until they give off their aroma, watching carefully that they do not burn. Immediately tip out of the skillet onto a plate. Set aside.

2 Heat 2 tablespoons of olive oil in the skillet. Add the onions and cook for 5 minutes, stirring occasionally. Add the garlic and continue cooking the onions until very soft and tender, but not brown. Remove the skillet from the heat.

3 Cut out four 12-inch/30-cm circles of baking parchment. Very lightly brush the center of each paper circle with olive oil. Divide the onions and garlic between the circles, flattening them out to about the size of the fish steaks.

4 Top the onions in each package with a swordfish steak. Squeeze lemon juice over the fish steaks and drizzle with a little olive oil. Spoon the tomatoes over the top, add a sprig of thyme to each, and season with salt and pepper to taste.

5 Fold the edges of the baking parchment together, scrunching them tightly so that no cooking juices escape during cooking. Place the paper packages on a cookie sheet and bake in a preheated oven at 400°F/200°C for 20 minutes.

6 To test if the fish is cooked, open one package and pierce the flesh with a knife—it should flake easily. Serve straight from the paper packages.